THE
RESTITUTION
OF
PROPHECY

by

ELEANOR DAVIES

Published by *The Rota* at the University of Exeter
1978

ISBN : 0 905617 10 6

The Rota is an independent, academic society,
wholly supported by its subscribers.
Its sole purpose is publication of facsimiles
of British tracts of the Stuart era.

This is the twentieth pamphlet published by *The Rota*.
For more information please contact
Maurice Goldsmith or Ivan Roots
at the University of Exeter.

Printed in Great Britain by
The Printing Unit of the University of Exeter

PREFATORY NOTE

Lady Eleanor Davies or Douglas (1590-1652) was among the most notorious, most confident and most persistent of the prophets who abounded in early seventeenth-century England. There was nothing remarkable in a claim to have a warrant from God to foretell future events — 'all saints have in measure a spirit of prophecy', said a fifth monarchist (Mary Cary, *The little horns doom and downfall* (London, 1651), p. 106, cited in K. Thomas, *Religion and the decline of magic* (London, 1971), p. 137; see also chapter 5, 'Prayer and prophecy' *passim*). Nor was it rare to take upon oneself the mantle of a specific biblical prophet. But it became a matter for comment when a high-born lady turned to soothsaying.

Lady Eleanor was a daughter of George Touchet, Baron Audley and Earl of Castlehaven. Her first husband was Sir John Davies (1569-1626), Attorney-General of Ireland and philosophical poet, author of *Orchestra* (1596) and *Nosce teipsum* (1598). Though Sir John was moved to write in praise of marriage — 'this cordial comfort of society' — their relationship was not a happy one. After acquiring the gift of prophecy by an anagram ('Eleanor Audeley' became 'reveale O Daniel'), Lady Eleanor foretold her husband's death ('John Davies' = 'Joves hand') and promptly went into mourning. He soon died of apoplexy, having just been promoted Lord Chief Justice for his amenable attitude towards Charles I's forced loans (1626). Her second husband, the Scot Sir Archibald Douglas, was himself addicted to signs and word-play — somehow he made 'Douglas' into 'duo gladii', a two-edged sword. He also had an encounter with an angel. Angering his wife by burning one of her prophetic writings, he suffered for it — 'escaped not scot-free' was her gleeful comment — and was suddenly 'bereft of his sences' (*The Lady Eleanor her appeal* (? London, 1626; No. 25 in C. J. Hindle, 'A bibliography of the printed pamphlets ... of Lady Eleanor Douglas', *Edinburgh Bibliographical Transactions* I (1935-8), 67-98).

The new Daniel's earliest foretellings were verbal. In 1626 she assigned sixteen years of happiness — 'that was long enough' — to Henrietta Maria, bringing the Queen aptly to 1642. In 1628 when there was a good deal of speculation about the prospects of the duke of Buckingham — his portrait fell off the wall of High Commission — Lady Eleanor said that 'his time' was not until August. John Felton proved her right at Portsmouth on 23 August. At once she was famous. Growing in confidence she predicted the birth of a strong boy-child to the Queen, confirmed by the arrival in May 1630 of Charles, Prince of Wales.

Family pride was one of Lady Eleanor's consistent characteristics. An anonymous correspondent in 1622 described her as 'mad, ugly and blinded with pride of birth', vowed to 'scratch a mince-pie out of her' and wished, 'the most horrible of curses, [her] to remain just what she is' (*Calendar of State Papers Domestic*, 1619-23, p. 400). The sensational trial and execution for rape and sodomy of her brother Mervyn, Earl of Castlehaven, made a great impact upon her. To the end of her days she saw him as the spotless victim of conspiracy and in her pamphlets, not least *The restitution of prophecy* (? London, 1651, Hindle No. 47), pursued 'the wicked woman', his wife, and her perjured witnesses. See also *Woe to the house* (? London, 1633; Hindle No. 3) and *The Word of God to the citie of London* (? London, 1644; Hindle No. 12). The Castlehaven case is discussed in detail by C. Bingham in 'Seventeenth-century attitudes toward deviant sex', *Journal of Inter-disciplinary History* I (1971), 447-472. From now on the prophet grew in eccentricity and arrogance. In 1633 her cryptic verses, apparently comparing Charles I to Balthazar and predicting a violent end for him, combined with the publication of other 'scandalous matter' by way of anagrams, brought her into the Court of High Commission, where she boldly argued with the prelates and councillors. The Dean of Arches, who had been doodling, suddenly interrupted her with an appropriate anagram : 'Dame Eleanor Davies' = 'never so mad a ladie'. Fined and imprisoned in the Gatehouse — it became Daniel's 'lion's den' — she predicted condign punishment for her persecutor, William Laud, unerringly identified as the Beast of Revelation. Her daughter, Lucy, Lady Hastings, the future Countess of Huntingdon, secured her release. But she could not keep quiet. At Lichfield, besides upsetting the canons' low-born wives by usurping their reserved cathedral pews, she profaned the high altar. Laud could not have been more alarmed. She was put in Bedlam for a spell and then into the Tower. Before she was set loose in 1640 she prophesied that London would be burned to a cinder. Sure enough there were some fires 'which frighted some foolish people'. Her freedom coincided with the collapse of the Laudian censorship. In the 1640s and early 1650s, in spite of the attempts of the various regimes to reimpose control on the press, she managed to bring out a stream of pamphlets and broadsides, mostly written in the astonishing 'stream-of-consciousness' style of which *The restitution of prophecy* is merely an example. Civil war and its consequences provided ample opportunities for new predictions and rehearsals of the validity of old ones. The British Library copy of one tract — *I am the first* (? London, 1645; Hindle No. 13) — bears a note by George Thomason : 'Taken a printing 17 Jan : 1644', i.e., 1645. In 1646 she was arrested and flung into a dungeon — 'hells epitome' — at the Compter, to lie among the rats. The very heavens, it seems, roared and flashed all night in sympathy. Like John Lilburne, Lady Eleanor was always ready to dilate upon her sad circumstances. By 1648 her eye fell upon Oliver Cromwell as a man with a mission. His initials, O.C., the sun and the crescent moon, clinched that. In 1649 she was gloating over the fall of Charles I, whom she blamed for her brother's and her own misfortunes. Many year before, she recalled, she had forecast his execution outside a banqueting chamber.

In 1650 Lady Eleanor had a remarkable encounter with another, not so aristocratic but equally scribacious visionary, Gerrard Winstanley. It seems that after the failure of the colony at St George's Hill, he and some of the Diggers were driven by poverty into humiliating wage-labour on her Hertfordshire estate. Somewhat 'near to herself' — like her father — Lady Eleanor was determined to get her money's worth and more out of the 'poore brethren' and argued with Winstanley about what she owed them. Winstanley in a superb letter denounced her as a false prophet:

> You said in Preston Barne, you were the prophetesse Melchisedecke, which is a high assumption ... Melchisedecke ys king of rightesness and prince of peace. Now if you be that divine power soe called, Then I say what means the lowing of the oxen and the bleating of the shep... Surely you have lost the Breeches, which is indeed true Reason, the strength of A man. And you must ware the long coates still, tell you know yourself' (P. H. Hardacre, 'Gerrard Winstanley in 1650', *Huntingdon Library Quarterly* XXII (1959), 345-9).

Unabashed she continued to prophesy and publish, still harping, (e.g. in *The restitution of prophecy*) on the insults to her family, mingling with them the evils of the times. Predicting 1656 for the Second Flood (*Restitution*, p. 49), she escaped that danger by dying in 1652. Her long-suffering daughter had her buried next to her first husband at St Martin's in the Fields, erecting an elaborate epitaph extolling their Christian virtues, including humility.

Later seventeenth-century editions of Sir Richard Baker's *A Chronicle of the kings of England* interrupt the history of the Commonwealth to devote a whole column to her passing. The reader is asked 'whether a person so qualified or so addicted might not with most equity be judged on this occasion to have been favoured with some beam of a

Divine knowledge of future things ... In the most flourishing conditions of the Nation' — the personal government of Charles I, 1629-40 — 'she foretold its unparalleled Troubles' (London, 1696 edn p. 617).

Copies of Lady Eleanor's publications, some annotated in her own hand, are held by the British Library — mostly in the Thomason collection — the Public Record Office, Worcester College Library and the Bodleian Library. *The restitution of prophecy* is Hindle No. 47. As with almost all of her works — *Strange and wonderful prophecies* (London, 1649; Hindle No. 35), the only one reprinted in modern times, in 1871, 1873 and 1875, is a notable exception — there is no printer's name or place of publication. The text is extremely difficult to elucidate. Biblical echoes abound, a few identified (e.g., from *Daniel*, on pp. 27 and 28 and *Revelation*, pp. 31, 37). The tract refers, often cryptically, to historical and personal events : e.g., the 'five years Fiery Bloody days' of Mary I; the 'unmatchable Reign' of 'her Virgin Sister' (pp. 6-7); Charles I's marriage to Henrietta Maria (p. 5); the execution of Strafford, 'no shallow Brain-piece' who 'had his *quietus est, Easter* Term (Anno 41). Sealed with no ordinary Arms, the Ax' (p. 25); the death of Lord Deputy Ireton (p. 26), and a great deal about her brother (e.g., pp. 8-25). She sneers at Laud's mean parentage (p. 32) and identifies him with 'the apprehended old Serpent' (p. 37). There is a reference to Cromwell putting on spectacles to read 'a *Book*' of hers 'Entitled, *Babylons Hand-writing*, bearing date *Anno* 1633' (p. 27). This does not appear to have survived. The subscription on p. 52, '*Fleet*', suggests that she was once again in prison. *The Rota* edition is reprinted with the permission of the Curators from the Bodleian Library copy (Collation : 4^0 : [A]^4, B-G^4, H^2. Pp.[viii] + 52. The first leaf blank. Shelf mark 12 θ. 1336 (4), Wing D2006. Wing lists, under Douglas, several items not in Hindle).

In addition to the references given above, information about Lady Eleanor Davies may be found in G. Ballard, *Memoirs of several ladies of Great Britain* (London, 1752) pp. 271-80; *Historical Manuscripts Commission Report, Rawden Hastings*, IV, 343-6; *D.N.B.*; *Huntington Library Bulletin* V (1936), 14 (referring to family letters in the Library); S. G. Wright, 'Dougle Fooleries', *Bodleian Quarterly Record* VII (1932), 95-8; T. Spencer, 'The history of an unfortunate lady', *Harvard Studies and Notes in Philology and Literature* XX (1938), 43-59.

THE
RESTITUTION
OF
PROPHECY;
THAT
Buried Talent to be revived.

By the Lady *Eleanor*.

John 16.

He shall glorifie me; for he shall receive of mine, and shall shew unto you.

Printed in the Year, 1651.

To the Reader:

THis *Babe*, object to their scorn, for speaking the *truth*, informing of things future , notwithstanding thus difficult to be *fathered* or *licenſed*. That *inciſsion* to the *quick*, hath under gone ; without their *Benediction* , in theſe plain *Swathe-bands*, though commended unto thy hands.

No ſpurious *off-ſpring* of *Davids* , but the *Son* of *peace*. This *Oblivions Act*, *Meſſenger* thereof. *Be of good cheer, O my people*, (Iſai.40.) *O ye Prophets*, ſaith your *God*, Tell her,

her, That her *Travel* is at an end; Her *Offence* is pardoned, our *Jubiles deliverance* : Sirs, to be plain, as in the firſt place, *His Commiſsion.* He firſt of the *new Prophet*; ſo his and hers both : She the laſt of the *old.* Confeſſeth likewiſe, or beareth record of his *preſence*, *Born in the fleſh*; of whoſe *Kingdom* no end.

Although not in a *Stable* brought forth, yet a *place* like *reſtleſs*; a hard choice between *extreams* or *ſtreits* of that kinde to diſtinguiſh. No *Inferior Priſon*, or of obſcure *Denomination*; whereof that ſtreet carrieth the *name* : not the leaſt, honored with no leſs then the *Temple* for one.

VVhere belonging to paſſages of *Inns*; The one frequented all Hours, and

and Drinking, not more free then the others darksom *grates close*; famished there no few. But requisit *Bridges*, and the like, the true *Narrow way* (by suffering) *that leads to life*: From him a proper *passage* or mention. Straits of the *Virgins-Womb* had passed; besides Seafaring-persons his followers in that way not unexperienced, afore arrive the *welcome Haven*.

And so far *Reader*, for these excluded their *Approbation*, where parallel'd the *Broad-way*, *Ebrieties* leading to destruction: Those *Gates* put into the reckoning, and such holds *chained* up, *&c.* and for this *nonplus* also; unwilling to transgress the bounds of a *Preface*, Shewing as by those *Vigilent Shepherds* (published)

lished) a *Saviour*: Their *peace* then required likewise a *pass* for these from ours, as appears, witnessed thus, *I give thee charge in the sight of God, which quickneth all things*, &c. *That thou keep the Commandment until the appearing of our Lord Jesus Christ; which appearing in his time, he shall shew, That he is King of Kings, and Lord of Lords,* (1 Tim. 6.) So in another place, *For the testimony of Jesus, is the Spirit of Prophecy, King of Kings, and Lord of Lords*, the Holy Spirits presence namely: But arrogancy begetting incureable *blindness*, these favored but as *non-scence*, not material. *Galio* cared for none of these *matters, &c.*

December 25. The *Fleet.*

Postscript.
But blessed is he not offended, &c.

Matth.

MATT: 25.

The Book of the Restitution of Pro-phesie : the great Account, &c.

THe *secrets of the Gospel under Allegories covered and Parables, precious Leaven, generality or scope whereof reflects, although on the day of Judgements severe account, unknown day and hours reserve :* Nevertheless, *days preceding their proper Lesson, a warning piece for them.*

Which Unum Necessarium *inesti-mable Pearl, the Kingdom of Heavens purchase, that Manna, the unknown Bdellium likened to : who sold all to compass it, requires Artificials none ei-ther, presumes cannot be frustrate, or by all troden under foot : of which an essay as ensues tendred, as to watch all*

B   *or*

*or wait :   ſo to beware if wiſe, how they
quench the Spirit, where not unlike his
dream of good conſiſted and bad, both
becauſe the thing Eſtabliſhed repealable
not, then their Decree, much leſs to be
changed,* &c. Dan.

*That conſiſts not in meat and drink
thoſe Externals, unto a wedding likened
ſo many Handmaids, his Kingdoms E-
pitomy at hand, or forthwith to appear
Virgins, their's the priority : five per-
fection of Numbers : Her quickning
time, till when concealed,* &c. (Luke) *a
prime period, alluding to the Sences.*

Five were wiſe, other five were
fooliſh ; *no lame ſimilitude, ten in number, its full time (as it were) or reckoning had gone out :* To whom how befel
thoſe that were out of the way, ſaying,
Our Lamps are out or quenched,

dreamt

dreamt not an anſwer that way inſuffi-
cient a point of what conſequence to ſay,
They had not thought or ſuppoſed, &c.
caſt in the teeth with Spiritual Chand-
leries an Item thereof.

   In what obſcurity all without the Spi-
rit manifeſting without contradiction as
appears : The Bridegroom while tar-
ried all ſlumbred and ſlept, bidden be
watchful : Therefore watch, for ye
know neither the day nor hour, *&c.*
as that for another, Could ye not
one hour refrain: *our caveat bids* ſleep
on, *who allow the Spirit not tranſmit-*
ted beyond the Primative bounds, what
real demonſtration ſoever, as if any
thing impoſſible with him : and thus the
blinde conducting the blinde, emblems
what poſture Synods and Church-men
found in : How provided of the wedding
      B 2   *garment,*

garment: *when that summons,* Come now for all things are ready : *The Spirit and Bride, saying,* Come, gates of Paradice wide open, no more curse, *&c.* the Tree of Life, *attain'd its Maturity, living waters* gratès Aurum Potabile *as free,* no longer to be fasting then.

And so much for their farewel rest-less good night, Lord, Lord, *&c. knows their voices as much as they dif-cern (read by them) the Prophets theirs,* &c. *unworthy of the oderiffrous Mari-age-gloves, or a taste of those transcen-dant Confections, even departed from the faith :* Depart ye follish Galati-ans, who hath bewitched you : *where-with verily, The Kingdom of Heaven expresly unto what* Nation *or* King-dom to be revealed obvious as those So-lemnities :*

*lemnities: under the notion of a Wedding, Revels not returnable often:
Whenas some supernatural anointings
or Conception, as by that Mid. nights
Alarm shaddowed forth, in due time administred: After the way of old illustrated, when the Word of the Lord came
unto them, Recorded in such a Year of
their Reign, and in what Moneth; pointed to a Jubile's moiety,* Five times five.
The years prime *Anniversary Feast,*
blessed throughout all Generations:
her VVedding-day, faithful Handmaid the Virgin *Mary,* her Five and
twentieth of the Moneth, as bears
date 1.6.2.5. Year of Grace: His
very Proclaimed Reign, Coronation accompanied with unhappy
Nuptials: He aged 25. she Fifteen,
&c. gracelesс voice, Twenty four
from

from the Conquefts Baftared Gene-
ration (comple at *Anno* 24.) matched
with a Yoak-fellow, and could not
come: five Yoke of Oxen of his
Oxford Commons an Item, muft at-
tend on her Ladifhip, roaring Sabbaths Mid-nights works : No Stranger fubject to be unmaskt, and Far-
mer Bifhopricks weekly Alarms.

VVhile fhe as free with her impo-
ftures to communicate our *Heavenly
Saviors* homage to Idol blocks doted
on painted Popets, for whofe name,
wo to the Houfe fuffices the Dogs in
the ffame place licking his Blood :
Moreover as in this Maps Circumfe-
rence contained, of unappy memory,
Her five years Fiery Bloody days,
of the name fuch knows none charm-
ing Letanies (*good Lord, good Lord*)
they

they know not what, *ave gratia*, &c.
Pater Noster and Creed alike intelligible, to her sorrow Matched in her
after days.

By her *Virgin Sister* succeeded, in
the Five and fortieth of whose unmatchable Reign was Interred at the
Virgins Annunciation, &c. those plentious times farewel ; The *Bridegroom
Sun* and his *Virgin Spouse,* parting the
hours ushering the *Obsequies.*

So proceeding with the subsequent
parable, whose Divine Nature as descended to a habit of Flesh : So by
this way of Domestique Affairs, unto the vulgar capacity condescends
the Kingdom of Heavens Title to
coroberate, presidents produces of
the present the fire Talents (to wit)
in what Reign.

VVhere

VVhere thofe three of no obfcure
quality : Their Lord as though returned from a far Country, had ac-
quired fome great Prize or Victory,
otherwife fome Merchants return.

Called in the firſt place a prime
Peer of the Land, fo highly preferred *Audeley* E: of *Caſtlehaven*, even
to hold up his Hand at the Bar, with
two of his Servants Arraigned and
Eexcuted all three on this wife.

He charged with the Rape, a Page
protefted at the laſt caſt, a Virgin
came into his Lords Service, and
went away a Virgin thence. The o-
ther an Irifh Papiſt, a Vagrant: The
Footman faid, had he thought Lords
of the Councel bade him fpeak for
the King, have ferved him fo, would
otherwife been advifed for his Pardon

Pardon called on St. *Dennis,* whofe
Oath taken contrary to Law and Iu-
ftice, refufing an Oath of Allegiance:
As Hers not at all, upon whofe Ac-
cufation before the Privy Counfel ;
taken away her Husbands life, that
in Court appeared neither that day.

Anne Strange Heretrix, of that
extirpated Houfe, Ifle of *Man*: In
which preferred Bill, this long Proces
wherein fhuned, Anatomized that
mankinde Grandams mery, and hers
like Daughter, *&c.*

As fhews in the day of his wrath,
wounding even Kings, *&c. Sit thou
on my right,* &c. thy Sentence (as
much to fay) until upon them be ac-
complifhed (*Revel.* 13.) *Even the
brutifh Beaft wounded in the head,* his
mortal wound : *And Hers* (*Rev.*17.)

*where one of the seven Angels which had
the seven vials* (namely the last of
them) saying, *Come, I will shew thee
the Judgement of the great Whore or
great bellied Harlot sitting on many waters* : The Cities Bridge on Arches,
this Map as displayed person, and
place, Circumstances none more ne-
cessary : And some Haven Town
from whence derives her Title of
Honor. So from the Title great in-
fers a Grand-mother. Then that im-
perious Hell-hound, more Mother
Jezebels then one.

And with the Holy Spirit moving
on the waters : Thus proceeding
dispelling Mists and Darkness, saying, *Wherefore dost thou wonder, or
marvel'st thou* (as it were) at this
Sea-Monster, not more strange
then

then true, *The Mother, &c.* I will
fhew thee the *Myftery* of the *Woman.* And the *Beaft* that *beareth* or
carrieth her, &c. Exprefly *Herals*
their *Myftery* which *demonftrates*:
And prefent *Century* the feventeenth.
*As behold whofe Arms? And they fhall
eat her Flefh and burn her with Fire,*
befides hers fome four-footed rather.
Skull, palms and feet, no Dog would
touch, in reference to *Feafts*. VVhat
Bruit or *Flefh* of Beaft in moft re-
queft, *Eaten, &c.* Points to fo many
Stags Heads born in a *Bend,* or their
Skulls, &c. Touching whofe *Arms*
fuffices fo much refer'd to *Sign Pofts*:
the *Red Deer* that Scarlet *Beaft* alfo ;
and *Babe* in its *fcrimfon bearing Clothe,*
a Relique to thefe days ; in her cufto-
dy : VVho cried out as much as fhe

(Gen.) him folicited daily:By whom his garment laid up, *&c.*

And fo what doft thou here *Elijahs enlightning days,founded* in whofe, Our Capital City *LONDON*, of old called *TROY*, A compound of *Babylcn* the Great : As written ~~Son~~ in her Forehead or Frontifpiece. VVhere from *His Greatnefs* or *Lord Mayorſhip*, not onely derived Title of *Great Cuckold* ; but Great *Britain* its addition ; fince exchanged *Anglia* for *Brute*,no lefs then undone, moft proper from him (one *change* purfuing another) embrewed in that way of his *Hounds* and reftlefs *Hunting* to prefer the Beafts name, accords but with his *Minions* that of *Buckingham.*

So running with him *Ahimaz*, The

The way of the *Plain* or prefent *Waveing Gothes, Sarazens,* and *Kni hts* of *Rhodes* out of date, and *Romes* fcituation remote : As they to their Father. See whether this thy *fons coat, &c.* whofe City on a River no flender one, with its Appurtenances (from which *Allegory* of carrying) *Ships* called *Bears* and *Tygers, Sea-Horfes,* fraught with *Tyrian* in *Grain, Pearls, Precious Stones, Gold,* and *Wines* in that abundance , *&c.* VVith Her Cup of poyfon arayed *Cleopatra* like, fitting on Seven Headed *Nilus* : The Beaft with fo many Heads and Horns.

The *Woman* and *Beaft* with fo many *Heads and Horns , &c. Church, Court,* and *Cities* defcription, with *Kings,* their obeifance to
her ;

her; befide in what *Century* : Alfo
his Seventeen years Reign, until
(*Anno* 41) Lead away not unknown,
by what means : our *Domitians* days:
in whofe, this City made an open
example : As behold whofe Bridge
fired, fhunning the *fire* to caft themfelves into the water, forced; Eaten
by *fifh*, their *flefh*. Since when others
fuffering, no few. The *Towers* Blow
for an other, with *Lightnings* and
Thunder-claps, like *Dooms-day, &c.*
the *Bridge* at the fame time Burnt :
when fhe no ordinary *Whore*, charged with a *Husband, Blood* : worthy
of no other *Cup, Naked* and *Burnt*.
Credible *Witnefs* of the *Churches A-*
poftacy, Figures in her later *Days* what
a faithful *Spoufe*; fealed with *Sabba-*
tical Heads of the Scarlet coloured
Beaft

Beaſt (*Cruelties Charaƈter*) with *Ox-ford* and *Cambridge*, no mean *Strum-pets,* whoſe Denomination interreſt-ed in the *Ten Horns* : Their *Tithe* an *Aſſembly* ſitting at *Weſtminſter* ; alſo carried by VVater in their Gowns, belongs thereto.

Furthermore, as this Cities Feaſti-vals and Funerals all ſet upon this reckoning, ſuch flocking then to be-hold her Pomp, ſtiled, *The great Whore with her Cup of Drugs* : Carri-ed in what State, By *Cerberus* Headed Hounds, her black Steeds. She ſit-ing on the *Waters, Her Habitation* or *Title*: By Kings at Arms and others, To give attention to *Preaching Pa-raſites*: whereas compared to the *Block-headed Beaſt* going to the ſlaughter. *Man in Honor,* as eaſie
for

*for a Camel to go through an Needles
eye, as for such to enter, &c.* VVhen
made notwithſtanding the Beaſts I-
mage : Laid before them : Adored
Obſequies for coſtly *Blacks* bought
at ſuch a price. VVelcome *Image*
of the *Beaſt, Saint,* or *Devil, Whore,
&c.* Honored a like, Sackcloth
when more ſeaſonable then *Muld
Sack* of late. Of which Sexes more
remarkables then one deceaſed.

So withal (part of the Bag and
Baggage) of *Saints-days* abuſed as
much by the rotten *Whore* : *Eaten,
&c.* That *Miſtreſs* of miſchief,
and her Servant the roaring *Beaſt*
wel-matcht : *Vermillian* Livery in
Grain, then *Simon* and *Judes* Commemoration : The *Floods* doings rather and *Sodoms*; crowed on both
fides

fides, as though never feen afore or heard their *Horn-pipes* attended ; whofe going by water retained to thefe very days *Trojean* Games : a world of Coaches, Belconies filling and VVindows, *Spectators* and to be feen ; becaufe *Jacobs* Flock fpotted, like *marks* by the foul *fpirit* fet on them : the *tokens* imitated, *Churches* by *Paftors* thus prepared ; a like for *Theators* and *his Temple. Varnifhed* with poyfonous *fpells,* or *paint* (fhe trodden underfoot) her accurfed *Pictures* ; or fome carted like dafht, *&c.* fit *Guefts, &c.* On the other fide *reftlefs-fwearing Cooks* about *Firs,* and other like *Catch-poles* ; appurtenances of the *Scarlet Beaft,* for this narrow *Table* too *voluminous* : Alfo *Chriftmas-boles,* All-nights *Game-*

boles ;

boles ; *Dancing* and *Dicing*, fcored on the *Horns* , with *Goldfmiths-ball* and *Skinners*, from the *Cup* of beaten *Gold* ; a *health* to them too.

Through whofe *ftreets* formerly carried in *ftate* by *Scarlet Liveries*, from all parts flowing to have fight of her *perfon* or *prefence* : Totally ftript of *Purple array, Margaret Pendants, Bracelets* and *Chains* : fome *Kings Daughter* as though , or *one of the* Blood : became as *deformed, difpicable* and *defolate*: Hated as formerly, followed with their *Leopard skins*, the naked *Houfe of Lords*, concerned not left ; befide plundered Pay : *Houfes, Kings* and *Lords*, thofe.

As moreover , *fhe* none of the left, that *mother* of *Witchcrafts*, branded for a Baud, whofe *Babel-Pyramid*

Pyramid fired. Fictions of fresh *edition*, *University Excrements* daily, whereby *oppressing Shops* and *Presses* with them : overflowing too shameful, whilest *Close-Stools* set to sale, lined through with *Scriptures old* and *new* : VVhen *Turks*, left *Gods name* therein, refrain to set their foot on a leaf of Paper, whose *Alcoran Mahomets* the false *Prophets*, *Cum Privilegio, &c.* Accursed *Ferocho's* reedified *Gates*, in the mean while *Ferusalems VValls*, waste, *&c.*

So sends greeting *Pathmos* Isle, to this Islands City. He when unexperienced in those *Hieroglyphick* Demonstrations *Saints* dayes, signifying beyond *Paganism* Rites celebrated. St. *Fohn* stricken or transported with such *admiration* and *marvel*

D 2   (O

(*O ſtrange*) and ugly: VVhat *Strum-
pet, Baud, &c.* As *points* to that *fiction:* of raviſhed *Europia,* carried on
the *Bull* into the *Sea:* true as the
others *Rape, &c.* in *Maps* and *Ta-
piſtries* ordinary; ſo to another not
long ſince no *fiction* on this *River.*
Thoſe Brace of *Spaniels, Her Graces*
ſwimming match. And *Knight* Er-
rand, no ſmall *Bull :* ſupported by
his Hand; laid upon her, *&c.* Re-
quiſit as any in our Cities Map to be
diſplayed. That *Eſprit* Order, con-
jured up again, entered in them as into that *Cities Swine :* becauſe the good
Spirit moved on the *waters* alſo *A-
piſhlike* by the evil *ſpirit,* and *Witches,*
thoſe, *&c.* VVith his *Venetian,* ſhe
free of the aforeſaid three *Stags
Heads ;* the *Horns* his too, *&c.* with
her

her *Cup* of *Viper Wine*, that never awakned, whether Drunken or no, *&c.* The *Floods* days not equivolent.

All which copied out by that *Piece*, when his *butcherly birth-day* kept, bound himfelf, *&c.* Inftructed by her *Mother Baud*, dancing her lacivious *Jigs* and *Tricks*: beheaded the *Baptift*; late by her, and her Ladies not onely Hermophrodite acting *mankinde*; but fworn by his *precious*, *&c.* And *wounds* by their bafe *Players*. *Let us eat and drink, to morrow is our laft:* More true then aware of, notwithftanding a *Mote* in anothers Eye perceive, fo returning to his laft account, made *even,* or *confefsion* on *Tower-hill*, arrived the *Haven* above. *This day be thou with me,*

me, &c. *Enter thou into thy Lord and
Mafters joy. Eafter* Term, *An. Dom.* 31.
Between thofe twain Sacrificed, he
charged but as an acceffary : Had
the honor neverthelefs, of firft entrance. Next Term theirs *Bradway*
the innocent *Page*, and the other,
&c. VVho in thofe times thought
full little of (*Jud.*) *Bradfhaw*.
VVhen thirfted after his *Vineyard*,
Mervin Earl of *Caftlehavens*. So
many *Manor Houfes*, to few or none
inferior : This *Kingdoms* forerunner;
or what fhould him befal : His *E-
nemies* likewife thofe of his own *houfe*
(to his laft) *fwearing* at every word
curfing, *&c.*
    This man never once charged
with *Oath*, other *then truly and verily* :
Taxt with *injuftice* neither, or owing
unto

unto any : Paid and rewarded all.

By means of alteration in his *Religion*, as much diſclaimed ; and miſmatching himſelf : ſcandalized by others *miſdemeanor*. They who worſt reproached him, was, *That he had the beſt things in him, of any man*, as well as the worſt.

Stumbled at the *Church* upon *point* of *Antiquity* : By reaſon whereof ſtood in *Poperies* defence, or *Romes*.

That *Fathers* aſperſion under-gone, *Origens*, *That when he wrote well, none could do better ; when he wrote ill, no man ſo bad*.

Envied among them, *Court* Moti-ons that ever diſtaſted, ſtiled to be *Pharoabs Son*, or accounted *the Crea-ture of Fortune* ; to whoſe potent *ad-verſaries*, no *ſlender* or *mean advant-age*.

age. Caſt by a *Fury* of Peers : His unnatural *Iury* of *Brethren*, a s ſold him, *figure* of the *Lamb,* called the *Dreamer* : ſcorned and ſtript of his *Garment.* Alſo between thoſe two, through her luſt. Blood of the *Grape,* as ſealed the ones *pardon* the life therein. So the other the heavy *Famins* forerunner hanged up : by Birds betokened on the *Wing*, his flight, *&c.*

In the end taſted *Egyptian ſlavery,* themſelves *Straw-gathers* : *Types* of the ſcattered *Jews* not onely ; but of a *ſpiritual Famin*, proceeding from forgetfulneſs, *&c.* Parables, conſiſting of a twofold-like *Conſtruction* ; as thoſe aforeſaid *Fellow-ſervants,* in one day ſaid to have their *Heads* lifted up both, who advanced ſo. *All knees to bowe,*

bowe, &c. **A**fterward biding them not be fad ; for their prefervation fent thither : So much for the word *throughout all ages*, and the *world* through. **A**lfo touching his leave taken at *Tower-hill*, fo highly rewarded. *Well done good and faithful fervant.*

Follows the fecond a Lieutenants turn next of *Ireland*, *Strafford* no *fhallow Brain-piece*, over-powered by the *old Serpents* policy. *Papift* by reafon in higheft *Offices*, had his *quietus eft*, *Eafter* Term (*Anno* 41.) Sealed with no ordinary *Arms*, the *Ax* : Neither wanting after his *ability* of what *Faith* or *Belief*, *Kingdoms* flippery places, as unto her a fecond *Eve* ; for her forwardnefs, ye know not what ye ask : VVhileft on the

E other

other side as backward. This piece interlined, as shews, when presented the *Lord General* herewith, a *Manuscript* prayed to be *priviledged*, by him referred to the *Bar*: Lodging in *Ax-Alley*, where about three *weeks* space waited on. Other *use* of which (as though) had not made, returned them, not vouchsafest the value of a word. No *Babe* in long *Coats*, though bewrayes, *barbarous* alike, not to *bless* where they ought, and to *contemn* or *curse*: No less then *cowardize* also in a high degree, what should be improved to *Hide*, *&c.*

In the mean time unburied *Lord Deputy Iretons*, sad welcome rung out, landed, whose *Corps*.

Farther giving to understand, had advertiz'd him what befel immediately

ately afore, signed with *Whitehals Powder mischance.* Bidden to shake of their dust, that have but *ears* for a shew : How in the same moneth *October, &c.* about the same hour at *Night, &c.* wherein delivered to *His Excellency* by her a *Book,* Entituled, *Babylons Hand-writing,* bearing date *Anno* 1633. Printed beyond Sea, by the same token with *Spectacles* put on, read by him. That *watch word* superscribed, *Is a Candle to be put under a Bed, &c.* (useless and unsafe) He that hath Ear hear this *Piece. Contents* of the said Book (*Dan.* 5.) contained in a sheet of *Paper,* sometime served on the late *K. C.* after his return from *Scotland, Anno* 33. Crowned, *&c.* concluded with *Charls* Be, from his name, attended

E 2   with

with his *Riotous Lords*, *Belſha-*
zer the laſt (to wit) *Beheaded*, *&c.*
to beware his *Banquetting Houſes ſa-*
lutation ; *Great Babylons* exchanged
Feaſt, into ſuch confuſion, inſtead
of *kiſsing hands*, ſtampt a *hand writ-*
ing, ſubſcribed, Great Britains *La-*
mentation Mourning and *Wo.*

VVhereupon like his *killing* and
ſlaying Decree, Dan.2. &c. She to
appear and *anſwer* forthwith, as by
that *Babylonian* reference annext,
Signed *Sydney, Mountagne*, for *pre-*
ſuming to *prefer* and *imprint, That*
deteſtable,&c. *An. Dom.*1633. *October,*
Whitehals no petty Treſpaſs.

Of which *Babyloniſh* Garment
hidden as it were in his Tent to this
day.

So much by the way for that, and
of

of his *Kingdoms* no delay admitting,
as by the forefaid *Advertifement* to
the fpeechlefs Dr. B*a*. B*alams* mad-
nefs reproved, when ferved or fuffi-
ced from thofe Ears. *Did I ever ferve
thee fo before*: put to filence by the
dumb Afs: all as fwift that way ; but
Midas Ears, their long Hair hides
not, or Perwigs either.

And thus in reference to the *pre-
mifes*, from a *Wedding*, its late hour.
That cry alfo after a long time his
return, of a cried *Court-day*. Officers
they called to appear, called *Thou
flothful fervant* Dr. Laud, as appears,
He the laft Arch. B. of *Canterbury*. The one Talent even buried by his hand, *Achans* gracelefs
Scholar.

In the Earth: he buried in the
Valley

Valley of *Achor* : a heap of Stones *Dunghil*-like ; his Monument and theirs confenting thereto : Had not alone troubled *Joshua*, expoftulating in *rent clothes* : VVherefore, *&c.*

Root of all Evil, filthy lucre con-feffes did covet : *Thus and thus, &c.* In the *Valley* of *Trouble*, took up his Lodging. Sign of the *Spade*, fitter for it.

And thus after a *verbatim* way, for our *hiding days* in feafon : Ser-vants fuch of *Mammon* or *Money*. *Weeping* and *howling* their Portion : Of the *Spiritual Calling*, or *Clergy voice*, as follows : Called *Thou floath-ful, &c.* One in ten theirs, reaped where *fowed* not ; gathered where had not ftrawed. A fevere or hard *man*, counted every *Sheaf*, &c. *Tythe gatherers*

gatherers (to wit) far and near, with
ufury ten in the hundred; not wanting their *Trade* ; known in others
Name.

In relation to whofe *Name* thefe,
even the *Beaft* out of the *Loathfome*
pit afcended (*Rev.*17.) *And they fhall
wonder whofe names not in the Book of
life, &c.* (or *Church-book*) namely,
That of *Canterbury* derived from
fome *Grace-makers* occupation, be-
low the *Dung-hils* office. As at firft
every *Creature* after its properly.

As hence appears how had occu-
pied, *&c.* That *digged and interred,*
fhrowded it in the ominous *Napkin*
to their *Napery* pointing, or *ghoftly*
array withal.

And one thus unfolding another,
as that *farewel* of his. Bidden, the *dead*

to

to *bury the dead*. Either becaufe *rich*
and concealed it, or might *allude* to
his *name* : In like cafe as *Canterbury*
or *Salisbury*.

The Title of *Grace Buried*, neither in *filence* or *forgetfulnefs*. That
Paradox for another, as implies.

His own bare meafure meted or
returned him ; he without excufe,
knew his *Lords* fevernefs neverthelefs : Lo there, *That is thine*, &c. As
from *him that hath not*, faying, *Even
that he hath fhall be taken away*. Of
Parentage obfcure, as much to fay,
His Gracefhip digraded fhall be (*Jan.*
10.) a day and hour not aware of,
to Preach his own *Funeral Sermon*,
not mentioned in his *Diary*. That
Fridays Chriftmas Cup, *gnafhing of
Teeth* : VVho hated the light, de-
pended

pended upon the former days *provif-*
fion, Star-Chamber Decrees and Ar-
ticles, was caft into the prifon of
utter-darknefs ; befides *Extortion*
added to *Ufury* ; *Covetoufnefs* very
Idolatry, alfo with *Gluttony* charged :
Emblem'd the *Napkin,* their ex-
cefs and concealed *Bags* ; fo of
which one *Talent* afsigned ; in fhort
thus, faying, *Lord he hath ten* : Dif-
puted as though fome other better
deferved it; anfwered, *He that hath,
more fhall be given him,* or *fhall have
abundance, &c.* Even *Anno Dom.*
1621. *Eafter,* (to wit) had the *fuper-
abundant* honor to be *the heavenly
Lamb;* ancient of days *Figure,* fore-
fhewing by a *Harlot Spowfe,* Remon-
ftrates not onely *Romifh Maffacres,*
that *Smoaking Clarret* ; but by *Pro-*
               F   *teftants,*

teſtants, how ? to the *brim* filled, &c.

VVherewith a word of the ſaid *Priſoners* preſent releaſe, by the figure *Ironia*, recommended, &c. delivered by *His Majeſties Chaplains*, His *gracious Meſſage* and *royal Favor* toward him.

He whereas was to have ſuffered as a common perſon ſhould die, now like a *Peer* of the Land, *beheaded*, &c. appointed to ſift him, no others admitted, having been under *Inquiſition* ſo long; upon their *information*, had thrice taken the *Sacrament* upon it, was innocent of thoſe *crimes* for which adjudged to loſe his life : whereupon thanks not omitted, replied, *Would eſteem it a coller of precious Stones ſhould draw him up to him,*

him, embraced the *Tree*, to his *Feet*.

And by thefe *Jews*, our *High Priefts*, in what *Execrable* maner *Crucified* on their *Altars*, prepared for that purpofe ; roaring with one confent, *Sacrifice* and *Eat*, both one, or indifferent ; alfo *Altar* and *Table*.

Like as in *Golgotha*, That fatal *Fridays* difmal day, (end of the week) *bowed then the knee*. *Chams* accurfed *feed*, by whom a *Giant-crucifix Goliah* like, not the value of a *Napkin* to cover, &c. Horrible to behold, *eclipfed light*, covered the *Ten Commandments*, under colour of an *Altar Hanging*, wanting no *nailing* either : Of courfe *Woollen*, *Purple*, *&c.* faftned down, left thofe precious *Tables* an eye fore.

F 2 VVhileft

VVhileſt mounted over the *Lords Table*, to kneel before it, with the *Centurion*: No *Dwarf* mounted on his *Courſer* or *Beaſt*, to be worſhipped to, ſuperſcribed a true *Copy*, brought over by *Father*, *&c.* in his *Holineſs* Chappel done thereby; *Lietchfield* Minſter for one, were forced afterward for fear of the *Parliament Forces*, thoſe *Clerk-Vicars*, to bury it in the *Dunghil*, not one would harbor it. As this added, the very hidden *Talent*, his *Lords buried Goods*, accords with the *Tables* of the *Law*, from no cauſeleſs jealouſie, as Extant in our *Bibles* ordered, except the Book of *Apocalyps*, and other like, leaſt edifying, may be beſt ſpared; allow others read every *Sabbath*, *&c.*

Beſides

Besides how many silenced imprisoned, other some *Crucified* on *Pilla-
ries*, whilest he and his *Panders*, eating and drinking with the *drunken*.
Item, *Oxfords* Roast, three hundred
Dowes or *Deer* at a *Chancellorships*
dinner, with *Spiritual Courts* abominable *Bribery* taking on both *Hands*
from those stripped of their *liveli-
hood*, *Widows*, but *Tenants* for life ;
no Commiseration for such, especial-
ly, present pay, or else turned out.

Unto which annext his *vow* of
Chastity, stiled, *Pater in Christi, &c.*
Verily, false *Christs* shall deceive
many, *whose names not written from
the foundation, &c.* (*Rev.*) Exchange
commodities; those *Virgins* Canonized
in his *Tables* admire, *Laud* his
name, *&c.* the apprehended old
Serpent,

Serpent, alias Satan, whose false *Keys,*
as though his *succession.* Iron Gates
opened of their own accord, were
in their custody (*Apoc. 20.*) *The Key
whereas of the sealed Abbyss,* whose
proper Seal.

And thus proceeding, a compleat
Fury, their *Verdict* with one consent,
Prophets and *Apostles ;* Touching
our *Nations story. English, Irish,
Scotish* and *French,* every one as
heretofore heard in their proper *Language,* fulfilling nothing so *secret* and
covered, that shall not be revealed
and made manifest.

Including withal *Times* reign or
reckoning, *Five thousand five hundred years compleat since the Creation.*
Secondly, *Two thousand years before
the Law, and Two thousand under the
Law.*

Law. Lastly, Compleat *One thou-*
sand under the Gospel, from those in-
trusted Servants account., which
would have amounted (had not he
faln short) to *One thousand* years
more, or had it not happened into
slothful hands. The *Three Ages* o-
therwise equally *Two thousand* years
unto each allotted.

VVhereof thus (*Apoc.* 17.) concerning *place, time* and *persons conco-*
mitants: Five are faln ; one is, the other
is not yet come: And when he cometh,
shall continue a short space : Namely,
the fifteenth century past and gone ;
the sixteenth bears the name, the other
not compleat to be, but shortned. Here
is the minde that hath *Wisdom*
(*viz.*) to number the time, *Psal.*
reflects on King *James* the Sixth.

Others

Others as weak as he wife, From
a *Parliament* called by himfelf, to
abfent *his perfon*, here fignified, *Of
one minde*, called by *write* ; others
by moft *voices, Chofen ones*. And as
rewarded for the moft part afterward, who hate the *Whore* and make
her defolate : A *Widow*, as much to
fay, *Utterly ſtript of all, by the Ten
Horns*, fulfilling fuch a time, a-
mounting to ten years fpace. As
moreover, *For God ſhall put into their
hearts, to fulfil his will*, &c. repented
as it were ; alluding to which words,
*Have mercy upon us, and incline our
hearts*, &c. or *Write thy Laws in our
hearts we befeech thee* ; where *aĉts*
againſt *Idolatry* and *Adultery*, made
death that *aĉt*, put into the *liſt* of the
aforefaid *ten Horns*, fo many years
fulfilling. In

And fo proceeding with his *rela-*
tion hereof, who wrote to her ftiled
fo highly, *The Elder, To the Lady*
Ele: &c. in our *Britifh* Language,
as to the full expreft, *Apoc.* where
accompanied with infatiable *Tyrant*
Times Myftery (*Eating all things*)
his difplayed *Arms* : alfo the *Stuarts*
Arms or *Coat*; The *Bulls-head* bla-
zoned, that fign in *Taurus,* giving to
underftand farther of *Europes* Apo-
ftate Churches, returned to *wallow*
in the mire, all from her fitting on the
waters of *Babylon*, with inlarged
skirts, thofe of *hers* as afore fhewed;
computed by the *floods* execrable
Age, *Hearts* as *Buff* : Signed and
fealed with *Babylons* Great Seal,
The Beafts heart : That fulfilled fe-
ven times, not to be Cancelled either.

How long afore his *reason* to him returned a *Jubiles* seven times seven, where included.

Lastly, VVhat affinity between them, fixt place as signified from her sitting posture, *&c.* So *restless time* by the weary *Beast*. Names written on both their foreheads, That *City Mistress* as upon Hers, *Mystery Babylon* or *London* : Also *Mars, Mercury, Venus, &c.* Names of *Blasphemy* on *his*, all *her most humble Servants*. The *Scarlet Beast, Anno Etatis, &c.* when her downfal withal.

By persons represented of no obscure *decent* : Namely, House of *Derby*, matcht with the House of *Oxford*, armed on both sides with the *Horns* : no *secret*, either he bearing the *Stags heads* metamorphized
into

into a *Bear* : Father of him who
suffered. On all *four* acting in their
likeness; and other of that kinde on
Stages in *Pastorals*, tumbling to the
admiration, *&c.* A *blessing* by the
mothers side : So *wherefore wonderest
thou at signs, &c.* *Rev.*17.

And sotish *Bathe,* another like
odium of the *Beast*, forerunners of
Great *Britains* unlucky derivation,
not onely from *Brute*, but of *Cities*
names their sympathizing, called
after theirs, or participating.

And so far for these literally pre-
figured , The present *Age* sent to
School to the *Ox, Ass,* and *Camel*;
In their *Litter* knows its owner ,
better observes the time , and for
times Mystery and *Seasons.* The
weaker *Sex* preferred more proper

for them, requisit for former days
neither : To whofe Difciples not a
little earneft (anfwered) *A thing not
in his difpofe, he was but the Word;*
but *his Fathers* where he pleafed, a
Conception; as much to fay, By *fpecial
Grace* : VVitneffed to be by them
though.

And fhunning *Circumlocution*,
where like theirs under terms *Enig-
niatical,* concealed by way of *Numbers* and *Figures* numberlefs. VVho-
foever underftands any one, ferves
for the *mafter Key* to that *hidden
Treafure* or *Quintefence.*

Of the *third* or *laft fimilitude,* as
follows, The laft days dreadful *alarm*
likened unto that *Sefsions* day, attended with a guard of *Angels,* by a
King fitting on his *throne* : On the
right

right hand faithful to *him* that stood
in defence of the *cause*; on the *left*
that took up *Arms* against him :
which *remarkable* days of ours compared to a *Shepherd*, *Jacobs* separating
the *sheep from goats.*   Our *Nations*
prime Commodity, *Wool, Sheep,* no
mean fence against *Hunger* and *Cold* ;
also pointing to such a *year* and *season*:
viz. The distance between the *Suns*
entrance into *Aries*, the crowned
Ram; probable when as the *Worlds*
Creation.   And that of the Tropick
Capricorn, the *Hoary bearded Goat* :
Character of *Spring* and *Winters* ap-
proach; whereby slaughtered sheep
as betokens an execution day, at
hand ; from the *fold* to the *scaffold*,
&c. So foreshewed to be the very
year, aforehand *revealed.*

His

His *finister* reign shadowing
forth from 1625. *March*, until his
arraignment after *Chriftmas*, the late
Charls his doleful *note*, imprifoned,
harborlefs, not worth a Houfe: A
Stranger (to wit) of another *Nati-*
on, where by way of retaliation as he
had clofe imprifoned others, un-
refifted *The bleffed Lambs voice*,
and *Decembers*, &c. Made it his
own cafe, in as much, *Had not vifited*
the leaft of thofe his Lambs, *Hunger*,
Starved and *Cold*: For any *mercy* on
their part, *Rebels* proclaimed to his
Kingdom, alluding to the *flaming*
fword; That *Doomfday* when they
expelled thence, whofe *Valediction*
depart, *&c.* The never departing
fword and *fmoake* their portion. The
Righteous on the other fide, or *Round-*
heads

beads pointing to *Paradice* their return to *peace* : As thofe *Thunder-claps* then, and *Lightnings, Auguſt* 23. *A*ᵃ 51.

So much for mittigating this *Mittimus* to *Hell*, expreſt by way of *Terror*, his *Judgement day*, the *Scape Goat*, no *Purgatory* pardon : whoſe Funeral attended with thoſe three, *Hamilton* and *Holland*, *&c.* made by them ; No private Account, Extends to oppreſſed Priſoners *Chriſtmas* Cry, Verily *Sterved* and *Rotting*, ſo over charged thoſe *Penfolds* ; under any *colour* or *pretence* buried quick, by accurſed *Cut-throats* daily, and imprifoned *Anno* 45. VVhoſe Twenty three years Reign, from *Anno* 25. until *Anno* 48. The *Scepter* when reſigned the Hand : *Table of bounty*

bounty turned to a *blow* ; as by the
Fruitleſs fatal *Tree Mythologiſed*,
of three years ſtanding afore came
under the heavy *laſh* ; beſides a
Leaſe of three years more ex-pired ;
Alſo a warning to *Churches*, his
Houſe, for uſurped *Keys reſignation*.
Enemy to the *Nations cure*, the
Tree of *Life* : *Scepter* and *Keys* both.
The *Epilogue* or *End* of which *ſub-
ject* or *excommunication*, concluded
with his *voice*. The inthroned *Lamb*
in *Bethlehems* Manger, concerning
otherſome in this *burthenſome age* ;
as unto thoſe groaning reſtleſs *Com-
panions*, overcharged by their unmer-
ciful owners. *Come unto me alſo ye
heavy laden, and* (your intolerable
Tax) *I will eaſe you*, and inſupporta-
ble Bonds, thoſe *Yokes*, ſaying, Be-
hold

bold I come quickly? Whose righteous-
ness like the strong Mountains, &c.
Judgements like the great deep, to be
manifested, *&c.*

Thus much for their *Analogy* or
likeneſs, unexpectedly alſo come
upon us unto the laſt great days account likened. And for this *Anti-*
chriſtian Beaſts ſevenfold names of
blaſphemy, namely *Saturn* and *Ju-*
piter, &c. Days of the week *chriſt-*
ned in theirs, and Moneths in their
commemoration Ethnicks; after *Julius*
C and *Auguſt*, containing VIC.
LVVVI. Thoſe *Members* no inferi-
or ones of the *Roman* breed, Hours
of the Moneth 666, whoſe number
alſo pointing to the days of *Noah*
1656. By ſo many Moneths amount-
ing unto 55 years and a half. Then

Treafure lyable to *Plunder* , of more confequence to count thofe at hand , including his reign of 55 years and odde Moneths fucceeded him , wounded not leaft by his begotten *Brutus.*

So then how paffes for current, or accords together, that fuch taking upon them to be qualified with *humility* and fear of *God,* do *prohibite fwearing* in others and *blafpheme* themfelves. Make *Laws* for ftrict keeping the *Sabbath,* notwithftanding fo ftupid and carnal, ftop the *ear* againft his *Word* and *Law, Thou fhalt have no other gods.*

VVhileft the *fimple* deluded by *affumed Titles* of *Saviours,* and the like ; called *Defenders of the Chriftian Faith,* An *Antichriftian* Authority

other-

otherwife called, *The Blood thirfty devouring Beaft*, rifing out of the *Water* in the *Lambs* Rofe coloured *Robe* ; wounded (as it were) with the Crown of *Thorns* : whofe *Baptifm* and *Sabbaths* exercife, edifying as their *Bells*, *Feafts* and *Fafts*, part of the Forty and two Moneths reckoning ; and *breathing* the *Holy Ghoft*, witnefs the three abominable *Frogs* for another ; with the *gift of healing*, *Miracles* by *fuccefsion*, the *Image* of the *Beaft* worn, *&c*. So of *Elias* A-larm, *Fire* caufing to come down, *&c*. (*Apoc.* 13.) in the fight of men by *lightning* as *burnt* fo many *Barns*, laft *Harveft* fulfilling ; alfo the *Harveft* great, but *Laborers* few : Put to their Heels for the Prefs then, not to be forgotten. Subfcribed I am *A*

& O, &c. And have the *keys*, &c.
As our *Liberty* proclaims; and the
Holy Ghosts reign for evermore,
sent in his name the *Spirit* of truth,
otherwise called *The Lamb*; likewise by their *Synagouges* how con-
fined within *Iron gates* : VVhose
Angelical presence signifies, as de-
clares, *He was in prison* ; *Depart ye
cursed*: *So blessed are they*, called unto
Lambs marriage supper.

Qui se humiliaverat, ipse exaltabit.

Ele: Da. & Do.
   Fleet.
  Candlemas.
Her *Purification.*
   1 6 5 1.

Principium & Finis.